Changing Your Story

Patricia Clark Smith

For Mark,

what a nice

meeting!

Best always,

Pat

(we need to
tape you + John!)

Changing Your Story

Patricia Clark Smith

West End Press

Acknowledgments are due to the following books and periodicals in whose pages many of these poems first appeared: *Southwest, A Contemporary Anthology* (Red Earth Press: 1977); *Voices from the Rio Grande; Bartleby's Review; Mountain Newsreel; South Dakota Review; New America: A Review; Cafe Solo; Blue Moon News; La Confluencia;* and *Talking to the Land* (Blue Moon Press, Inc.: 1979).

First edition, January 1991
ISBN 0-931122-61-9

Cover art by Norah Flatley
Back cover photograph by Margaret Randall
Design by Michael Reed
Typography by Prototype

West End Press • P.O. Box 27334 • Albuquerque, NM 87125

Contents

For these:

Josh and Caleb
Shaula and Max
Anastasia, Maria, Kirsten
Lori and Misty
Brian and Stephen
Rafil
Anthea and Gwendolyn

I

Traveling with Friends

CLOSING DOWN

for Warren, Ellen

December sky all day.

A pewter bowl clapped down around my town.
Now, ringing metal air of desert night.
Sounds carry; all serene,
traffic from four blocks away.

I am a solid faithful woman.
My hands, trust them,
do what they think they ought.

The ritual precedes, outlasts
the reasons for it.

Look, I have made an advent wreath,
ivy and evergreen from the back yard,
white candles, walnuts, and bright tangerines.
This morning I spent
scrubbing the tubs down clean,
blue powder and hot water, and
this afternoon I cooked.

Thick yellow chicken with loose skin to brown,
carrots and garlic, thyme,
and mushrooms cleanly sliced,
red wine to make the sauce get dark and thick,
and clap the cover down.
Coq au vin.
Air of the house still brown and heavy hung.
The guests have eaten, gone,
the children, you, asleep
under your blankets, orange, blue, and green.

My neck aches from tending,
listening toward Advent.

Something coming.

When?

I want to get up now, put on my coat,
and take a widow's walk around our town,
pass silent by the bars on Fourth Street,

blocked shadows under arches
of great roads north and west,
dark libraries, closed stores,
graveyards, wreathed houses of the dead,
and tumbleweed balled up in vacant lots.

Pass by, pass by
all the town's houses, rooms
ringed with the peace of breathing,
children in their deep sleep, insensible
now to the headlight beam that shoulders in
and swings around the wall to check them out;
old people dreaming by a waterglass
with bubbles coalescing on the edge
toward dawn.

ALBUQUERQUE SUNDOWN

Albuquerque sundown, and the clouds
boil up greedy, block the west,
lightning swaggers pink and thick
in whole webs, or bright two-second blots
beyond the city, above the five volcanos
which Roy tells me aren't dead, not yet
(somewhere down there, lava lightly snores),

and wind rises, rushes up in big loops
through dog city, where somewhere tonight
their satanic majesties the Stones
all loose lips and little asses are playing

At Uncle Cliff's Family Funland
where the orange lights go around and around
on all the wheels of all the rides
the children cry for pleasure, for fear
as night deepens, crowd thickens
and merry-go-round babbles skater's waltz,
coins click in change machines
hooked like swords to rideboys' belts,
while lightning licks, leaps,
and the mongoloid boy goes around and around
sitting still as a doll in a toy boat
holding his all right sister's hand
two eyes like blue sieves

looking to strain his mama's face
out of a circling soup of faces
looking out for the single look that says
yes all right be quiet and good
as a quiet egg
and smile won't you smile

I know where I am
I dream places like this
and a bad dream circles inside my skull
like a fish in a bowl
as the miniature train
the pinball machines
sing don't trust do not trust
the roller coaster to cleave to its track

like lover's mouth to lady's body
everything sometimes turns indifferent
do not trust that the crowd will not suddenly turn
and gates be clenched tightly as teeth.

JEMEZ PUEBLO: DECEMBER 26

At Jemez, at the crêche, we go to pray
or else leave money if we don't know how.
The baby is a doll, the room is bright.
Nothing is empty here, no niche unfilled,
no corner of the heart not occupied.
Bright shawls and blankets, tinsel, Christmas lights
and cotton snowballs dangling from long strings,
good popes and spacemen, martyred presidents
picked out in iridescent colored yarn,
a Santa Claus with eagle feathers on,
ojos de dios, deer heads, paper plates—
like Dante's rose, like Arab drawing rooms,
like Chartres, like them all, or none of these.

Wherever one may sit on the long bench,
that is the center, and our host explains:
Long time ago, the world was very great,
and not like this one that we know at all.
First everyone was good, and then got bad,
and so the waters came to flood the world.
Everyone wanted for the child to come,
and see him, there he is! Sit down and eat!
And for the day, we too are taken in.

And so I eat beside my Jemez friend—
so newly friends, discovery of ourselves
hangs in the air between us like a dove
that might, in panic, pluck out both our eyes,
or else continue feeding from the hands
we reach toward one another—
Eat, then, at the long table, out of bowls
and, first and strangest, eat blue cornmeal bread
thin as a promise that might not be kept,
as promises that were not kept and tore,
and melted on the tongue as they were made;
venison chile, hot enough to burn
the tears back in your throat, and grape koolade
to drink in memory of—well, what you will.
This is the meal the gentle women set
before us. Giving. Gift. I cannot talk
in English or Tewa. What's the word
will serve for "thanks," or "sorrow," or "to bless"?

ROAD SONG: NEW MEXICO 666

Driving
rented car
reservation roads
I know ten words in Navajo
sik'is   my friend
yah anianaah   come in
and dusk coming down in country music
Merle Haggard
allout longing

Me too
wanting twenty grazing horses
winter doormat coats
red black cream
to look up
to watch me by
wanting someone
wanting you
hands in your pockets
to be walking the snow near Sanostee turn
where late sun clips Bennett Peak
shapeshifter mountain

Your hands
your face would be cold
I would stop for you
with no surprise
I would let you in

APOLLON

In every photograph I have of you
you squint, bright bronze and ruddy brown,
leaning against the sun.
A little drunk.
In fire.

No images of me.
Light meters wouldn't work, the places I've been.
Crashing through brush
I wandered in the king my father's wood.
Alders branched all alike.
Dark ragged poles of tamarack,
blueberry bushes scraping at my thigh.

One year, last year,
I bumbled out of shade.
Six, seven paces out into the light
and I came lightstruck:
blue eye seared and hard.
Yucca spikes snapping clear.
Mica glint cracked off rock.

This year,
electric in April,
your voice burns on hot wire.
Fat insulation sizzling off my heart,
tequila burning down, and touch,
your talk like knifeblades.

This is the summer when I love the sun:
gold wheatfield by Laguna, sunbit skin,
mica to flash in all that glinting rock.
Now in July, adobe courtyard bakes.
I drink Jim Beam, slouch in a canvas chair
in Albuquerque in New Mexico.
Bantams and Plymouth Rocks
and pheasants, both the silver and the gold,
churr softly. There in the gander's yard
twin sprinklers spin:
Guiltless guiltless guiltless that water lisps.
Whiskey and water. Birds, and children in the sun.

Afternoon deepens out in sinking fire.
Through my green scrim of courtyard cottonwood
West Mesa hangs out, glowing chile red.

Myself grown incandescent, somehow these years,
and dangerous enough to cast a shade.

Night falls, in stars.
Feverheat; even a sheet too much.
Murmuring charms in telephones:
We'll burn each other out.
Hang up. Lie in the dark and grin:
Let it come down like sun.

Wake in white dawn
dreaming a litany to crash like sun off rock:
My lover.
Cup of gold.
Sun-fire man.

FORTUNE

for Ana, for Bill

The old solutions work as well as most.
Turned pauper for a night, or day, or days,
being a woman, I make soup.

Parsley is dollars.
You chop those lacy greenbacks fine
with onion, rank silver,
and little coins and big change—
lentils, and carrots thickly sliced.
I say, lie there and simmer.
Make me a treasure pot of gold.

I turn the kitchen radio up loud.
Ronstadt comes on with "Crazy Arms." She knows,
man's woman's voice,
thick as good whiskey, good stock going down.

My son says read me, read me *Richie Rich.*
I do. His eyes grow wide as quarters:
a castle playhouse, kindly dinosaur to guard the estate,
butler who bursts last-minute in
to save the bloodroot family jewels.

Bright-haired man, come back,
or come back when you can.
Soup does not fill me up,
not even children, mockingbird in the yard,
sun hanging low, copper on cottonwood.

Listen: last evening, mosquitoes thick,
I walked the ditch bank with the kids.
Fish jumped. We leaned on rusted rails
and watched the sluice gate roil off blurs and gouts—
ditch water, green as gardens,
go spilling back into the Rio Grande.

Younger kids raced ahead,
but one child, not my daughter,
mashed her tight lovely face against my ribs.
She cried, *This is the time of year things fall apart.*
Holding her over water, what could I say?

Some things. Not everything.
Ana, young otter, our sleek silver girl,
be rich.
Friday we'll get our ears pierced, walk so fine,
walking so bright and swaying handsomely,
even the men who love us now
will turn, and turn, and sigh.

Walking back, looking out for younger ones,
toward grown ones waiting in the fading light
who couple, break apart, dance as they must
(Ana, one day recall I'm one of those),
by that dark ditch
thinking, my golden man, man shut in a dark house,
by that dark ditch I then began to sing:
Well you drop a silver dollar on the barroom floor
And it rolls
Because it's round—

I love you.
And you know how that song ends.

COMING BACK

for Susan Dewitt

June storm clouds blowing in from Taos Mountain.
Ten miles away across dry sage and sand
rain palace builds:
gray ragged pillars rinsing down
to slake the valley. Sun shines slant on us
still picnicking, but wind
a rumor bruits along the eastern slope
of piñon ridge, cold, loosely circling.
Soon.   *Soon.*

Pack up kids, friends, and stumble for the cars
and hit the road before it gets washed out.
big drops mean business. Bounce
along the ruts sheepherders' wagons made.
Sagebrush scrapes metal doors and undersides.
Jackrabbits spook
in splendid hoodhigh leaps.
                              This hot stale air
inside the car tastes safe. My little son
squirms on my lap to get a better look
at where the rabbits go. A day should end
like this: Amazing Grace
we sing, and take the bounces hard and clean.
The next car eats our dust. We're heading home.

Main road. Hard dirt.
A pickup slows, stops, signals us to stop.
Old couple, hollow, slackened throats and jaws,
but eyes bright as nickels, staring in.
We'll do, but only just. I know the look.
How much
an acre did we give, where from,
how long, how many, name and job and age
who do we know and what?
Be sure the kids stay clear of rattlers,
neighbor's boy killed two
a few days back a little ways away,
and glad to yes be seeing you drop in.
I speak to them as to a microphone;

a public broadcast. Let's get out of here.

A mile clear of their tallying and talk
and we spot something humping in the dust
they left behind.
                              A broken snake
heaving himself in arches, tying knots,
trying to unwind his beige and golden braid.
The belly plates gleam pearl
except where blood seeps red along the seams.
Undone. Undone,
his agony a shield to shut us out.

Here, where all other things cohere,
color to colors, cloud to sky to rock,
hell's idiot rhythms hold him.
He jerks at angles, jerks and tries to rear
straight up in air or bore directly down
in dirt, his chosen path
no longer horizontal secret smooth
past choice past any motion making sense.
Not venomous, not this one. Only big;
now monstrous. Thrust and jerk. We cannot bear,
and cursing we back up and run him down,
crushing his head to make him quiet, flat,
more for our sake than his.
                              Sick, looking back,
I see him lie like rope along the road.
A few more drops and then the wind lets down.
Dull sun, limp air.
The storm breaks somewhere else, and we go home.

MY UNCLE'S NAME IS JIM CROW

My Sioux uncle
keeps his stetson on
inside the house even

he sits in green fatback chair
in my warm living room
and makes crow calls

from his wide hands
holding invisible harmonica
he makes one crow caw
second call back

and warm house air
smelling like radiators
cooking and cigarettes

is cracked wide across
and we are walking

wide white field
someplace in Dakota
fanned with black scrub oak

black birds flap
crack coarse jokes
over our raw coming

snow's going to fall

MEETING UP WITH THE PICARO

for Tony

After all those months of slowed heartbeat
shallow respiration
I still mistrust the wild loops of blood
rushing up to my cheeks when the phone rings
and it is your voice

your forces aligning mine
iron filings swirling into place
beneath the big magnet

Sweet mover
tender hustler
hawk on the lookout
operator of the galvanic battery

it's no safe energy field I've stumbled upon,
but I tell you,
good things are happening:

when I buy a new notebook
instead of pebbled black cardboard like always
I walk off with red leather,
ruby and smooth against my palms
the poems spill out to swell it full

and dressing to meet you
I put on red wine velvet
slide my fine rings back on my fingers
silver bands about my wrists
I hang eardrops that make noise

My hair shines, electric
and my body's a carnival
a Mexican wedding
paper flowers pasted all over
horns honking weaving up Central
a whole string of reckless drivers

HERMANO

for Marta Weigle

Como fuistes enganado
Hombre despierta y advierta
Entre las horas del día
Te asercas más a la muerte
          —Penitente notebook, Rio Arriba County

North of here, Rio Arriba
Holy Thursday, some time before dawn,
up in those mountains you might find something.
Say you are the village idiot.
You are the scholar.
You are in the middle of life.

Your legs are sticks, thick and unused.
They cramp in the kneeling cold.
One light is moving away from the *morada*
and you are the man who follows the light.

Bobbing. Delicious.
It is there to follow,

and after a time it floats off the track
on down Cañon Embudo.
A long stalk, then.
You follow it.
You follow for miles.

You carry a knife.
You are thinking of things to say if you have to:
"I was hunting rabbits in the moonlight
I must have the wrong room
I took the wrong turning . . ."
But, *¿Qué dices, hermano?*
What has anyone left to tell me?

You are shaking like an owl's feather
when the sudden winds stream up the *cañon*
and that light is not put out.
Your feet slip, slide on loose flint
trap-clattering off, out into dark,
and only when the last stone is quiet

16

will he stop and wait.
He will turn to face you.

Tu hermano de tinieblas.
He knows he knows you to the bone.
His grin gleams broader than all your dreams.
Ten ivory spindles brush his robes aside
and inside his rib cage, a candle stub.
You suck in air. Pulse,
poise of that flame.

Once he is gone, you can go home,
cut wood for your fire, sleep warm in your bed.
But always now you will remember
all your sheep have skulls.
And you; you know where you are going.
There is a wagon you listen for.

Or go back to the city, if that's where you came from.
Doing up dishes,
touching your lover,
odd moments, it takes you.
Light bursts inside the bone chandelier.
Dimly, in the kitchen,
drinking tap water from an old glass,
your wristbones shine through,

and often at night
the freeway a *cañon*,
chaparral on both sides. Your tires strike,
skid on loose flints.
All the winds stream down.
A single light mocks up ahead.

SOME RESERVATION VALENTINES

Roan mare breaking morning ice
pawing the pond near Many Farms
her colt hanging back
waiting to drink

at Red Rock even the creeks run red
slow blood veining out against the drifts
sandstone
windworn to tables,
needles
now in full sun making lace out of snow
I chant to myself

Chinle red   Chinle red

At Rock Point Cato beats the drum
sound moves through my feet clear up to my heart
we sit in a circle
and we are singing
Dził nizhoni
I am coming to Beautiful Mountain
it's a woman's song

Alice Tsinajinnie grins
with no front teeth
red flowered skirt
plum velvet blouse
red striped anklets above her keds
Valentine woman
she stands up
and says she'll sing one
her soft cracked voice:

sugar in mornin
sugar in evenin
sugar in suppertime
be my lil honey
I love you all the time
hey ya hey ya hey ya

hey

SAN LUIS, NEW MEXICO

for David Remley

At San Luis, on Good Friday
they reenact the crucifixion.
¿Como los penitentes? No, señora, nada de sangre,
no blood, a light cross.
Three hundred yards from church to chapel,
small crosses like children make for pet's graves
to mark each station.

The Christ is twelve, with a speech defect;
a few years ago, a lame boy did it
and now he walks. This one may yet find his tongue.

It's the old men's day. They know all the verses.

And what is it for, out here in the shadow of Cabezon,
with the spring wind making the dry grit go
in the clear hard light near the unblurred edges
of New World rock?

The parents, the relatives back from Los Angeles,
up from Albuquerque for Easter weekend,
take polaroid pictures and embrace each other.
In this town they touch, the flesh still more real
than the snapshots of it,

looking up when Veronica stumbles forward,
wipes his face with a towel, shakes it and shows
the miracle, embroidered agony,

and the Mary who is no better than she should be,
dressed in whorehouse black, lovely twelve-year-old limbs,
comes on to lift the boy man she loves
with a world awakening on her face,
and she knows, she knows how lovely she is
as she helps him toward death and Sunday morning.

SHADOW

Once, you edited a chapbook: the oral history
of three teenage unwed Latina mothers.
You handed me a copy and explained,
Women in pain are what I care about.
Soon after, you dropped out and disappeared.

And you returned. For months, you ranged the halls,
thin shadow with bared teeth
ducking in stairwells, edging around corners.
You sought out classrooms where women spoke,
women with soft voices, long dark hair.
You'd huddle in a doorway, listening,
and there you'd batten, gather bulk.
Then you'd burst into that room,
unfurl a Penthouse pinup, scotch-tape it to the board, and scream,
You women!
You think you're such hot shit!
But I'm the poet here!
Your black raincoat swirled about you
as you nipped out the door
and no cop ever came in time to catch you.

I was your decoy, your betrayer.
I spotted you, I dialed the hotline number,
then I walked up and put my arm around you.
Sit down and talk with me, I said;
You said, *I can't, there's too much energy,*
and so we paced the hall together.
Behind your back in secret
I felt up that K-Mart bag you always carried
as gently as I'd ever touched a lover,
gauging if it held a knife, a gun,
a length of pipe. All I could feel was cloth,
and crinkly paper. *My poems!* you said, and beamed,
patting my hand that cupped the wadded lump.

In words both true and not I said
I often think of you,
I need to know how you are doing.
Your shoulders twitched,
thin shudder like a cat's:

You said, *I have this problem,*
a hole inside my heart, a real big hole,

but Dr. Christiaan Barnard, even you,
you must have heard of him,
he'll operate and fix it down in Houston,
then I'll get down to writing,
I'll show you all!

The cops came. I said, Look, I'm sorry,
but you turned brilliantly to face them
as if they were your Ph.D. committee,
with your good-student's trick of putting profs at ease:
Sit down, sit down! We have a lot to talk about!

Though you were sick, there was no place to hold you.
Released, you just kept coming back and back,
angrier now,
more confident.
Until he hurts someone, the state kept saying,
we cannot hold him.
Only the Navajo medicine man would help us.
I don't know what that elder did exactly,
but he assured us we were safe;
the medicine was working backward now.

Slowly you faded, sure enough. In time
you made your way to Thomas Merton's abbey.
You told the monks how you longed to see God.
They gave you food,
a little money for a bus back home.
You only got as far as Louisville.
You said you didn't need the monks,
you knew how to mortify the flesh yourself.
You fasted on those streets until the day
you dragged yourself up to the clinic stairs,
your liver so diminished you died there,
in bed.

Often these summer days I think I glimpse you,
back in the cool dark of some used bookstore,
entering Burger King as I am leaving,
in high stacks of the library, or crossing Central
at the next light, just up the road.
But you're not after me.
It's not your poor ghost makes my breath catch short.
It isn't you,
just something about this world.

NANDI (THE CATTLE POEM)

Delhi-Bangalore-Madras; for Judith Kroll

1.

One hundred twenty degrees,
a late monsoon.
No one can be certain of any harvest.
At late afternoon in the slanted sun
workers come heading home from the fields.
Children and dogs go running to meet them.

They come walking in pairs:
men with men,
woman and woman,
bullock by bullock.
Rice flour mandalas drawn by women
before every door at every sunrise
scuffed back to dust by cattle hooves,
soles of human feet.

Grandmas, aunties, big sisters cook outside
over small fires. The hot air shimmers:
garlic, turmeric, pepper,
onion, woodsmoke,
chapati baking on heated stones.

The very feeble, even the dying,
all stir and raise their heads:
someone is coming

The mud walls of houses grow gold.
People call this *the cowdust hour.*

2.

In any city
you think it must be a Western woman
clacking along in high heels behind you.
When you stop to rest, a she-goat trips past,
her hooves precise on the concrete walk.

After the rains
in the vacant lot by the Agra Hilton,
water buffalo,

they who have no sweat of their own,
skins shiny as vinyl,
wallow and snort in their bright green mud.
From across the hotel wall
human sounds drift of splashes, shouts,
the sprung thump of a diving board.

The street kid milks the cow on the sly,
when the dairy seller turns her back.
He aims the teat straight down his throat,
two quick squirts,
and ducks back to his friends
wiping froth from his lips.

The cow rolls her eyes.
She says nothing,
nothing.

And at the place of Gandhi's burning
bullocks are mowing the wide wet lawns.
Sweet green grass arcs
are thrown off the rotary blades behind them,
and all night long
in the park across from the embassy
the beggar sleeps sound
pillowed on a bullock's shit-smeared flank.

Cows stroll the neighborhoods by themselves
all day on business of their own.
People smile at them.
My friend tries to explain:
You see their eyes?
They are mothers, like us.
Even the men cows are like mothers.

At the intersection,
Radhakrishna and South Beach roads,
a cow stands beside me.
We wait for the light to turn.
It's a hopeless jam,
an overturned cart, two wrecked autorickshaws.
Exhaust swirls around us. Every horn is honking.

I place my hand on her neck.
I accept her judgment.

Together we make our way
in dignity through dead angry traffic.

3.

People paint cowhorns in careful stripes,
scarlet and cream,
black and yellow like hornets,
mostly green and orange;
this means *we remember Nehru,*
we loved Indira,
we vote the Congress Party,
a South Indian bumper sticker.

All the cattle go hung with bells,
bells the size of a baby's toenail
strung on fine wire
and wound about the painted horns,
middling bells to stud the harness,
clankers bigger about than onions
slung from fat rope halters,
and then brass caps to fit over horntips,
little pagodas to catch the light.

We ask Suneethi, *Where could we go*
to buy that kind of stuff the cows wear?
and she says, *To the cow adornment shop.*

At his dark stall in the village bazaar
the shopkeeper speaks only Tamil;
we ask Suneethi please to ask for
one set of cow adornments apiece,
horntips, bells in all gradations,
everything short of harness,
the works.

Suneethi frowns.
The shop man gestures.

The whole street presses close to watch.
Something is not going well.

She turns back to us,
He asks how many cattle you have
and I told him you come from New Mexico

where the cowboys and other Indians live
and you live on ranches of many cattle,
but he says you must not buy
adornments for only two of your creatures
because all the other cows will feel sad.

We say quickly,
Tell him we keep only one cow apiece.

He does not believe us, as well he should not,
but he outfits us, nonetheless.

If I could, I would tell him the truth:
Listen, we keep no cows at all,
in my country the streets are given over
to metal, to the flattened dead,
all the cows are imprisoned,
none go adorned,
and I buy these bells only to remind me
of a place where I lived once with animals.

BLUEBERRY HILL

for Dennis Jones

The last night I saw you, we were dancing,
it was Fats Domino, your good grin bopping
above most of that crowd. The wind in the willow played,
the moon stood still. Always
you were graceful who thought yourself awkward
in your West Texas accent, your long loose body. I see you
teaching, laughing, fishing,
scooping up a child. Dennis, how well,
how sanely you loved this world.

We said goodnight, see you maybe at Christmas,
though all the vows we made were never to be
you would send me the name of the young Kenyan writer,
I'd have Joy sign her new book *In Mad Love and War*
for you by next summer.

And now this morning the story long distance:
you dropping incredibly dead
with Beth your true love by your side
high on some Norwegian mountain, a blueberry meadow
where they don't pick blueberries one by one,
drop them plink plank plunk down into a pail
the way Yankees do; oh no,
those Norwegians break off whole twig-ends,
slurp them deliciously through their mouths
and swallow great dusky clouds of berries.
This impressed you,
you, always a man easily thrilled. Dennis,

you are part of me still,
and I imagine how it was,
you sort of dancing, your arms flung wide,
gold fillings glinting in alpine sun
and crying out just before you died,
how can we be glad enough
for such abundance?

II
Born to Swim

THE GREAT PAT SMITH AMERICAN DREAMPOEM

I have been teaching poetry too long
I know this
everyone else thinks so too
the trick's to clear out before they say so.

In a dream I am leaving
crossing Central Avenue
wider now than the Rio Grande
heading down and west
past Jack's and the bloodbank
past Gizmo's and Blazer Finance
saying hello
to my sad downtown that was always waiting

I am taking a job
becoming the best cashier in Albuquerque
my register sings
I call out orders:
sunnyside up
once over lightly

I smell like french fries and Evening in Paris
my nails are polished
my smock is pink
my hands drip nickels

all the regulars call me Patti
spelled with an i
they eat me up
while the juke box plays
Lacy J Dalton
Willie and Waylon
I hum right along
I know all the words
I am cashing in

One day my customer is Busby Berkeley
He leans on my counter lights his cigar
looks me up and down
likes what he sees
and says in a wise voice
Girlie, can you swim?

I show him my medals for the 400 freestyle
the 1958 First Annual Pine Point Maine Open Water Classic
He says Esther Williams is making her comeback
They are calling the movie Born to Swim
If I meet him tonight at 8 at the Y
he'll let me audition for the chorus

Suddenly it is all so simple
there are no limits
to all the colors light can turn water
my stage name is Tammy Aphrodite

I am one of the girls
we swandive from volcanos and Grecian columns
stroking tandem, we angle down
then bubble up like spangled lilies
slim fish   chlorine virgins
who cares about tenure
I lose the need to breathe
I could stay down forever

In a world all light and water
I am the wet,
the wordless angel

IN THE SIGN OF AQUARIUS I AM MAKING BORSCHT

for Janet Adelman

All this dark afternoon, to read and trust
for heat to draw good broth from herb and bone,
leek, bay and carrot, thyme.
Outside, snow thickens on Sandia Peak.
The pot hums *skim me,* and this house smells home.
At dusk chop fleshy leaves and cellar roots,
cabbage and beet to turn the kettle red,
swirling royal as robes around my spoon.

Janet, my January-born,
this is our time of year.
Irish-Micmac-Canuck and Russian Jew,
we make damn poor Aquarians, me and you,
whose gifts the old books say are great and cold:
keen second-sight of ages not yet born,
love universal, not particular,
the pure serene of intellect,
high air. Fixed stars.

OK, those too. But also we make soup.
And memory stirs. Again
I knead your pale warm back and count your breath;
across your belly's arc
my eyes meet your man's eyes,
longing to drink your pain until your son at last
dawns surely from between your shaking thighs.
That afternoon your three-year-old and I
walk home through Berkeley streets.
We swing locked hands,
shout out his favorite song:
> *Solidarity forever,*
> *Solidarity forever,*
> *Solidarity forever,*
> *For the union makes us strong!*

Tomorrow is your birthday. I make soup.
I make believe
you'll sit down at our table here tonight.

SURVIVAL LETTER TO PAULA

for Paula Gunn Allen

You again beautiful vaudevillian
homing back from up north, from playing the Micmac,
reading those poems you make up someway
out of grace raw meat

Head thrown back on a cushion
brush back your black hair:
I'm goin' good for an Indian girl
these last two months
I've slept with one Asian,
one black and one blind guy
the twist of your mouth
I laugh
choke Coors clean across the room

and tell you about my Navajo students
Díne ridin' high while I drove their school bus
air conditioner out and wanting a beer
with red rock and roll coming off the tape

Res-ervaTION of ed-ucaTION
49ing songs, they knew all the words:
Doo yaa shoodi da
biligáana
always something slightly skewed
in white man white man
biligáana biligáana
—You get that one, Pat? they call from up back,
—Yeah, sure. (Sweat. Downshifting fast,
highballing down La Bajada Hill.)
That time I made songs in my head:
me Snowwhite
me drive Rosered

Good drinking good talk
poems and men
and playing the old games. Someday we say
two breeds on a quest
we will seek out the wise old Anglo man.
We will know him.

Whole reservoirs
great gates of water
gleam in the tail of his wise white eyes.
He is drunk on vision
mad with Old Charter
blowing smoke from a chimney in four directions

Grandfather we will say *teach us how to see*
Daughters he will say *my sweet sloe plums*
laying his hands somewhere about us
mumbling of mirrors
lasers electricity

Laguna lady my darkblood friend
better drunkards you say than watered fools

Tonight I dream you show up at my door
summer night like this
wind out of the west and Scorpio rising
Antares starheart pulse red as rimrock
locust earthchild down by the river
nightchant sifting down from cottonwood
beyond this valley your mesas waiting
and gods the woman ones are walking
Tse-che-naku Changing Woman Grandmother Spider
fullbodied wideminded they stroll the high ground

they want us strong, Paula
with a clean welcome
they take us on
laughing

III

Changing Your Story

IN THE REGIONS OF ICE

for Margaret Randall

"I'm glad you can cry," you said,
"I can't seem to feel a thing. My lawyers
are dancing someplace, I hope
I'll feel something sometime soon,
before the tv crews get here."

Margaret, I love you. I am remembering
myself tonight, a child in Maine,
those deep winters, how they hurt.
Really, we did walk unplowed roads
more than a mile from where the school bus left us off
to home. This is the corniest
of all American stories. My sons laugh, sure, Ma,
and yet they know it's true, about cheap boots,
our thin coats shipping water.
How we urged one another on,
swinging our arms, singing forbidden songs:
Luckies taste sour
Just like Eisenhower! and
One hundred bottles of beer on the shelf,
One hundred bottles of beer!

I remember how it felt when frostbite
would start in, when your snot freezes,
me and my brothers, our friends getting numb,
our fingers, our feet growing slow and thick
as blue spruce trunks. One of the little kids
would always want to lie down in some field
to make snow angels. *No*, we'd say, we older kids,
Come on. Stamp your feet.
And we'd aim for those shafts of light,
a lamplight across blue snow, just getting home,
whatever that meant to each of us.

                                        At last
we'd make it to our moms,
the smell of our own kitchens,
liver and onions, applesauce, creamed cod, baked beans,
potatoes bumping up against the pot lid.
And then the stink of our wet wool: socks, mittens, coats,

our leggings set to steam behind the hulking stove.
Ice chunks dripped on linoleum.

                    How gingerly
we'd put our feet, our hands down in the washtub
my mom filled from the kettle. Almost
we would prefer the ice, the being numb,
the bravery of our act of getting home
to home itself, home where each finger, each toe hurt,
as the slow blood, the feeling seeped back in.

I'd look across my hot mug of soup
or cocoa at my brothers,
my mom's face.
The clock would inch along from half past four to five,
beyond. My dad would be home soon,
skid up our road in the big angry Ford.

                    I'd think
of all I'd really have to deal with then,
and soon,
and after that.
And after that.

ALLOUETTE

I get born first into a world of women:
Grandmother. Great aunt. Mother.

Julia crushes cans beneath her thick old lady shoe,
she kneads pale sweating oleo
into gold lumps, picks tansy, peppermint
in our back yard. She feeds our sopping clothes
into the dangerous black wringer, sets them aswim in air
along the squeaking pulley. She never sits,
except the times she rocks me, *Frere Jacques*
and *Allouette, je te plumerais* she sings,
Quebec still nasal in her country voice.

Anna, her mind gone simple as water over stone,
fathered by the same priest who christened her.
She watched her washerwoman mama die, screaming, drunk,
and scalded like a lobster in her tub.
A fireman wed her once. He stayed two weeks.
She needs what luck and love she can attract
so she burns incense and fat votive candles
and keeps a Buddha statue in her room
beside the crucifix and virgin.
she reads her cards and tea leaves. Sometimes
she kisses me all over, so hard I cry,
but that's a secret. Evenings,
home from Prophylactic Brush, she teaches me
to spell my name in pennies, P-A-T,
and makes her simple magic:

> *Two little dickey-birds sitting on a wall,*
> *One named Peter, the other named Paul.*
> *Fly away, Peter!*
> *Fly away, Paul!*

Always, those paper birds come back for more.

Rita, my rare mother,
slim as an iris stem
in iris-flowered prints with padded shoulders,
bobby sox, saddle shoes.
She telephones from work each day at noon
to say she loves me, to say she will be home.
Luminous in the bath she shares with me

until the day I reach for her, admiring,
Your pussy is so soft!
She can't imagine how I know the word.
Listening to 78's, dark summer rooms,
Sinatra, Woody Herman, Lady Day.
Heat lightning freaks outside.
The blackout curtains belly out and in.
She's writing V mail to a photograph.
He's all the men there are. Someday he's coming home,
back to you Rita and to our little girl,
so those thin letters say she reads to me
the way she reads me tales of how the Prince
finds Sleeping Beauty,
how Brer Rabbit gets home to the briar patch.

Julia, Anna, Rita,
my first, my three strong queens.
Softly they sing to me,
Allouette, je te plumerais!
Je te plumerais les ailes—
Pretty skylark,
I will pluck your wings.
This is a teasing song
my people sing to children.
I'm the pet skylark swooping through their court,
feeding from all three hands.
I do not know that nothing is a game,
how skylarks' wings get plucked,
how birds do all return.

I do not guess how soon a strange man's voice
will shake our sunlit rooms, *I will by Christ*
brook no spoiled brat!
Jobless, for months he slumps
wearing Air Corps fatigues, missing his buddies,
huge presence in the kitchen
sighing up all the air.

Rita and Anna keep on going to work
while Julia cooks tightlipped, no longer singing,
banging the pans around,
thumping her pail against the mopboards while she scrubs
elaborately around him.

He hisses *Matriarchs!*,
slams out to buy a paper for Help Wanted. In years to come
he'll tell the family history upside down,
how he came home, and what he found there,
and how Thank God he got back just in time
to save us all.

SOME LESSONS

Northampton, Massachusetts, 1951

Mr. Woods came to school
four times a year to give us
nature talks.

Weekends,
my dad and I walked the reservoirs,
Quabbin, Mount Tom,
hunting the moccasin and copperhead because
he said they killed off baby ducks.

So by third grade I knew
blacksnakes weren't slimy
or poison and I volunteered
to hold Blackie even before the boys.
I shuffled his soft coils
from hand to hand like cards
not worrying for once
which was my left,
my right. I let
Billy Keefe and Bob Dunphy hold him too,
and Judy August backed off ten feet
at my advance.

Knowledge is power.

Fourth grade was different.
Mr. Woods came without
a sack of snakes
or nests or milkweed pods.
He sucked his cheeks in and looked sly.
He asked,
What is the closest factory to us?

I knew that answer cold.
I couldn't even wait to raise my hand.
I shouted, *Prophylactic Brush,*
and they're on strike right now!

No, he said, *you're wrong.*

Other kids, pleased,
guessed places even further off:

39

Livingston Woolen Mills,
Oneida Silver.
No, he said, and *no.*
Do you give up?

We did.

It's this green plant
right on your teacher's desk,
we call it phil-o-DEN-dron,
it manufactures oxygen,
the air we breathe,
and that's why we call factories plants.

We all turned restless,
having been cheated.
He said, getting firm,
They both make things.
They are the same.
No one disagreed.

And I went home to where my maiden aunt
grew aspidistra,
snakeplant in her dark room
she shared with Nana
and her statue of Ste. Anne de Beaupre,
who could make miracles.

All week she smoked and cried,
spiritless union maid.

In bed I listened while
my family talked money all night long.

SKATER'S ELEGY

for WRN, 1922–1971

Ice Capades, western city, matinee.
One pair of skaters for a moment turn
one perfect motion,
and here, in the dark arena,
my mind brightens, blurs,
widening northward now, and back in time
25 years.
Boston, Springfield, Lake Placid, and I hear
Harry James' honey climbs and aching easy slides
on "Sleepy Lagoon,"
your song, Uncle Walter, for whom I could not cry,
and you and a woman, beautiful, your wife,
are slurring fields of green and azure ice
in limpid curves.
Honed.
Oh, together and apart you glide
like two leaves caught by choice
in spiraled updrafts. There must be some unseen
and secret center you, she, turn around.
Somehow, a child, I know
you make the image for some one thing so fine
I won't know what it is for years and years:
this near approach and brush, pursuit and heel,
this whirl and touchnot, only almost, almost,
until at last my breathing rises, breaks
in praise at final lift and leap,
together now, moving as one, as one.

The rest is much too usual to tell.
Real walking's hard once you have mastered ice.
Your feet go flat and wooden after that;
ground will not speed you.
The girl you married off the rink becomes
a woman with your name, and whiskey makes
a sound like silver hissing in your mind.
One day the fragile plain on which we skim
breaks and betrays you fully out of grace:
"Olympic Skater Dead at Forty-Nine"

and I am back in my own time and place
with children at a shoddy spectacle.

Frozen your memory again.

Only, I think how in November now,
in western Massachusetts, where you lie,
the mallards will be gone from Ashley Pond.
Crayfish and snapping turtles all lie deep,
burrowed in mud.
Cold air.
Hunter's moon.
Pond water glazes, thicks,
and bittersweet, a fierce, scarce orange, twines
up trunks of brown oaks, burns,
now all the leaves are gone, against dark pines.
Snowclouds will mass above the Hampshire Hills,
snowscud blow off Mount Toby, Sugarloaf, Mount Tom,
and one day soon
sky will grow dark and flat as smoked plate glass
and clean snow spit and whirl, drift and lie still
over a graveyard that I've never seen.

Here in the West, the mindless dance goes on.
You're two years dead.
I cry for you at last, and think
how polar expeditions sometimes find
sabertooth, mammoth, iced in a glacier's side,
of movies that I've seen
where frozen beasts are thawed and come alive
to stir and stalk the snowfields for new prey.

Listen, my Uncle: tonight I dream
I find you in a dark and quiet rink
frozen inside a cake of blue-grained ice
big as a county jail.
With my warm hands, my breath
I dream I make old winters melt away
and shard by shard dissolve the glaze and rime
of marriages, lost jobs, forsaking friends,
mumbled disgrace and doctors, ruined flesh,
all fallings-off, until again you stand
alone, recovered, body bright as mail,
your arms extended, waiting for the cue

that sets you free.
Inaudible music—go! and one last time
make the performer's gesture, circle clean
around the rink's edge.
Then be on your own, and, like a planet, wheel,
cutting across the reflex of a star
beyond my pity, memory, my love.

FOX WOMAN

for Julia Larock

What can I say to that man
when he says I am killing him?

When I was his child, foxes denned in his woods,
living off field mice, wild grapes in the summer.
They stole his chickens.
Now they eat me instead.

I could tell him that's why I don't come home,
but he would strap me hard for a liar.
He would try shooting foxes the way he does,
aiming for shapes
triple-tracking the snow under a cold moon,
and again he would miss, blaming crooked barrels,
though grandmother knew what happens to some girls,
and anyway, listen:
this is her story.

It is winter
fox weather
and I am the woman covered by foxes,
one the soft blacked silver of city snow,
two bright as tangerines.
Their pointed tongues flick like bad neon

as they work me over.
One coarse brush laps across my mouth,
two blanket my thighs.
Foxbreath smiles in and out,
smells of hot, faint wine.
These long nights
moving toward solstice now
their hunger quickens,
and I am the woman who lies down with foxes.

When I rise,
my sides intact,
I am Fox Woman:
she.
My den smells of me when I wake at night.
I walk the streets of Saulte Ste. Marie

and look like a woman.
All but one fear to track me,
one man at a time,
and he is young. I know his name.

He follows me into that bar,
brushing snow from his hat,
snow caked on his new boots,
and maybe I am sorry for him,
but I give off musk. When I turn to him,
I have yellow eyes.

ONE FOR JOSHUA

Home again from camp,
you walk the garden edges by the wood
searching for squash bugs, signs in the jimson weed.

Your brother trails behind.
He is the serendipitous one,
and more unfair than he could ever plan.
You missed seeing the rattler killed at camp,
but he is first to spot the fallen bird,
cecropia moth on bark,
although he skips and does not walk
and seldom goes without a stick in hand,
whacking in rhythm to some easy song.
He makes them up:

> *Solitary solitary rock rock rock*
> *The cows love the chickens*
> *but the cocks do not*

Dirt loves him as its own,
leaps to his skin.
The natural.
He is the charmed one dancing down our drive
who would eat all our hearts, were we not wise.
(You were the first to warn us; day he was born
you drove your trike into the road
and parked there, waiting for some truck to take you down.)

And you. Your heart was born to break
over dropped flies, a Dallas loss, your pride.
Yet you were born perfect, your one odd mark
dark speck in your green iris,
a mote in one pure pond.
I loved you first because you stayed alive
though born to me, whose goldfish always died.
Where did you learn your grief?
(I think of crazy Steve,
his whiskey burst into our hospital room,
all those pink roses and loose flowered gowns,
shouting, "Let's see the Baby Jesus!")
You take on our sorrows.
Your brother sings.

And yet how many times
out of my mists of anger or despair
I've seen you, your arms fierce about each other,
glaring at me like one child, and clinging in a way
that's sure to save you both.

Lately you say *remember* to each other
about a lot of times I was not there.

Yesterday, you find the runic alphabet
in one of my old books.
On the hottest day of summer you lie on our brick floor
writing your thorny messages to one another.

Joshua and Caleb.

ᚱᚲᚨᛁᚺᚲ

This word is brother.

ᚱᛉᚨᚠ

This word is blood.

Brothers,
my sons.

THE CRANBERRY POEM

a recipe for Josh and Caleb in New Mexico

Start with these garnets,
glowing in plastic bags stamped Ocean Spray
from Massachusetts Bay saltwater bogs
where berries bob like lifeboats in the breeze
blown cold off currents down from Labrador.

I used to find them wild, at home in Maine:
our swamp
fringed round with tamarac,
blueberry, bittersweet and alder scrub,
those pisspoor woods the redwings loved in summer.
A quaking bog,
swamp starting to dry up,
upholstered over in tough sphagnum moss,
and undulant beneath my lightest step.
It was waterbed walking,
walking across the place where water slept.
If you broke through that fiber mat, you plunged
hipdeep in black November water,
your whole leg going numb,
and all around
the stink of old swamp giving up its ghosts,
gas bubbling from whatever ripened there—
bones of the fox or copperhead,
tadpoles who didn't make it, belly-up,
the rotting native dead.

I walked that bog in my red rubber boots.
My thirteen-year-old body blazed with secrets
making me fierce to stalk alone.

Cranberries grew there, scattered, rare,
never enough to gather for my mother.
Bitten, they made a bitter meal,
shocking as true valentines,
the taste of heart in mouth,
but then, those years, there wasn't anything—
chokecherry, sprucegum, sourgrass, boys—
I wasn't wild to taste.

A quarter century's gone down,
and in New Mexico tonight
I teach you cranberries.

Look here. You chop them coarse, so some stay whole.
(Meat grinder's best, the heavy kind,
clamped to a kitchen table, hard enough
to scar the wood.)

Stir in some grainy sugar, not too much,
and last, some orange peel like Nana used,
like her grandma did when she could get it.
Backwards, we tell the names from you to her:
Caleb and Joshua,
Patricia,
Rita,
Julia,
Narcisse,

and then one more.

No one recalls her name, only a shape,
vast as all Canada,
that waddling woman, cook for the logging camps,
dressed like a man, they say,
trousers, rope-belted,
flannel and wool and furs against the weather.
They say she never spoke,
but her red blood,
it pulses strongly down my tongue tonight,
imagining her for you, that no-name woman,
stirring a bowl of cherries.
Lamplight
and the smell of kerosene,
a logging shack outside St. Simeon,
the wolfwhite winter banks of the St. Lawrence.

I'm a woman in high desert with no daughters.
Now in my hardest winter, I learn most clearly
how much it's worth,
all things we three remember,
all spirits we three raise.

Caleb and Josh, remember
cranberries chopped up coarse,

sugar and orange peel.
Set it aside to ripen for a while,
and go to bed. Tomorrow we give thanks.

My body older, warm beneath the quilts,
still aching after what there is to taste,
my fingers stained by cranberries to wine,
and you two growing taller in your sleep.

I dream of berries working in the dark.
Beyond our roof,
the stars of autumn wheel; toward dawn,
Scorpio sprawls across the whole horizon.
Antares, his one red star, it blooms and blooms,
that fiery berry, garnet red,
and ripening through ages at his heart.

FOR MICHAEL, WAITING FOR HIS FIRSTBORN

March 20, 1982

1.

Michael, my brother, Mike,
your name a litany,
one I still sometimes whisper into dark.

We hunkered in your room when we were small.
In summer, those years, hurricanes angled north,
killing the rambler roses with salt spray,
beating young corn down flat,
and making all the windows belly in.

Our parents stormed below,
swirling through the tense downstairs,
unleashing the bad weather of their hearts.

Us trying to shut out voices in the wind,
our arms around each other,
and you, the younger, saying *It's all right*.

All our fierce childhood long,
wordless, we told each other that same story,
our household tale:

Oh, let them fight below,
that angry woodchopper, his bitter wife.
We are in the forest,
two children driven forth.

This bedroom is our cave,
and pirates, or the kind mute animals,
the bear and fox, will take us in,
show us where springs arise.
We can live well on purslane,
dandelion green.

Should they come after us,
you be the tree
and I'll be lichen growing on your bark
and should they try to chop us down
I'll be a quiet lake
you be the silent carp beneath the water's skin

and should they try to drain us
we will transform ourselves again, again,
to quiet things.
Oh Brother, hold me tight.
We're seven leagues from where our father rages.

2.

The tv cast blue campfire light
while we watched Twilight Zone,
Have Gun, Will Travel,
Death Valley Days.

Deep voices sang:
O hear us when we cry to Thee
for those in peril on the sea
and Paladin, Paladin,
where do you roam?

Later, gone forth in truth,
you voyaged like we always said we would:
Da Nang
Marseilles
Karachi   Panama
the blue gulfs off Oman.
I stayed on land
watching the tv weatherman,
only a guess, sometimes, where you might be.

Once, when the whole Atlantic heaved and bucked
you headed your frail tub into the swells
and held her steady only by your hand.
Riding it out.
No radio, no sleep three days,
Liberian registry,
two hundred miles off course.
The company never called to say they thought you lost,
but Lloyd's of London met you at the port.

You told me three years later,
us drunk on margaritas in New Mexico.
I cried.
You said, "You just keep calm.
You bring her in."

3.

Michael, survivor,
tonight your child lies cradled on the sea
beneath the breastbone of your greeneyed wife.
Her small fists curl and uncurl like the seaweed,
grown quiet now, and waiting to be born.

For her this week the planets move
into the rarest turn of their great dance
that happens once in centuries:
Mercury Venus Mars our Earth,
Saturn and Jupiter, aligned.
I wake my sons at three.
By owls' light, we huddle on our stoop.
We look up at the stars
and say, maybe the baby comes tonight.

Her family, too, aligned,
waiting tonight to bring her safely in.

Planets and people.
If we have influence,
let her be quick tongued, loving, unafraid,
earthy and joyous. Yet let her have the grace
of knowing that all of us,
all men and women die.

Shaula Marie,
named for the startip of the Scorpion's tail:
the bright point of it all.

(Note: Shaula is the Arabic name for the last star in Scorpio.)

CHANGING YOUR STORY

for JAC

Listen, Jim,
here is the story I want someone to tell me:

Once, a girl had seven brothers
who went out hunting.
When night fell, they did not return.
An evil witch had changed them into swans.

Next morning she, who shared their blood,
cried out, "My brothers wheel about the castle!"
They had become more beautiful than men,
and yet at once she knew them for her brothers.

Seven swans lit on the parapet
and gabbled out their tale about the witch
and of the counterspell that stupid hag let slip:

Your sister must be mute for seven years
and knit you seven shirts of stinging nettle
with her bare hands; then, you may go free.

"Will you do this for our sake?" the eldest brother asked.
"Yes," she replied, "I will."

"All right, that's well," they trilled,
"only you must remember,
a single word has power to undo us,
and now we must fly south.
Sister, farewell!"

"I will keep faith," she said,
but she was speaking to the empty air.

I think perhaps her magic task
was only one event
in the long history of her silence.

Silver nettles grew behind the cowshed
where snails tracked spittle in the moonlight.
She used to hide there with her brothers
when they were children all together,
to whisper secrets,
to get naked,
causing one another to transform.

She gathered pricking nosegays
until her white hands blistered,
and thus she too grew webs between her fingers.

For seven years she worked and bled
and kept her counsel.
There was no easy explanation
for her behavior.

Girls who bake bread from seaweed
can say they do it for the science fair.
Girls who put a drop
of menstrual blood in tea
can claim they're doing it
to charm a lover.

She fashioned clothes of nettle
and she said nothing
until at last
even the king who'd wed her for her quiet mien
had to concede she was no normal woman.

By this time, seven shirts were done,
all but for one left sleeve.

On Saint John's Day
they stood her on a pyre in the square
and lit the faggots; even so,
she never dropped a stitch.

Just when her very hem began to smolder
wild trilling filled the air,
and those stunt pilots,
those hotshot swans,
divebombed the flames.
She flung the shirts out, one by one,
and one by one each brother
touched down to earth,
a man restored.

All but the youngest,
handsomest of brothers.
all his days,
a swan's wing billowed
from his lefthand shoulder.

They say he never married.
They say he always called her on her birthday.
They say she loved him best of all
for the swan-mark he bore.

Brother,
that is the tale I want someone to tell me,
this one I'm telling you now.

But Jim,
there is no witch for us to fool
and no spell I know how to break
when you call me dead drunk
the last day of the year
you who have lied to me so many times,
to tell me you are dying,
to tell me how I must not tell a soul,
not one.

You say you know how,
if it comes to that,
I'll go with you into those final woods
and hold you close.
You say you know
I'll have the strength to pull whatever trigger
and make a good clean shot
and cover you with leaves.

Some things, you say,
are understood.

Then you hang up,
and leave me speaking to a rush of wings
beating across the miles of empty air.

DREAMING THE BEACH

for Caleb

1. *Off Baja; January, 1974*

When they whelp
the whole beach reeks of death,
as if those bearded papas,
Darwin, Freud,
joined in a final nightmare
of warmblood infancy.

An island beach off Mexico
where elephant seals, the crusted males,
weigh tons,

the fathers' faces, yard-
long muscles
thrust erect.
They'll challenge anything,
bachelor seals, the kids,
the empty air.

Idle,
they loll and boast.
They roll.
They crush one pup in three.

Mothers
are dazed and vague.
Pups shriek.
Death is not quiet where
the injured linger on.

A mother seal may nose
flat carrion, or her own pup,
pinned, broken-spined,
still making noise beneath
its father's bulk.

Mama's mild and dumb,
confused, a little curious
at best. She's
a lover, not a fighter,
as they say.

There where survivors flop and fan
themselves among the dead,
black buntings rise up,
settle down again.
The flies adjust.

And some of us must speak
about our human childhood,
our father's rage,
our martyr moms
who seldom saw ways out.
My mother,
saying with her sad eyes,
her sweet clenched lips,
Honey I always hug
you when you're near
what can I do except
not notice much of what
goes on and I can't see
the way to live without
him baby mine keep
quiet stay well
out of the way sweet
dreams I love you

Maybe we'll all get by.

2. *Punto Año Nuevo, California; April, 1985*

All I can see is surf,
the sand and wind.
Redwings seesaw
and call from reed to reed.

The grown seals have swum out
to feed off continental shelves.
They won't be back for weeks.
Spring tides have washed away the dead.

Home free.

Now is the time
surviving youngsters rest,
pumped up on lactate
thick as buttermilk.

At dusk
they practice in the shallows,
vast adolescents
trying out their moves.

Mostly they sleep.

This wide trail
ends in a sandy hump
not dune or driftwood.

I fear him dead
until he spasms,
big sneeze, his snot
swirling like lariats. My sight
awakens: this whole stretch
of shore a dormitory,
kingdom of sleeping young.

Most of them will make it through,
begin it all again.

At ease,
alone, asexual,
and safe for now, a tribe of kids, they dream
maybe ahead to herring, squid,
backward to mother's milk
or looming heft and blood,
a fatherweight evaded
just in time,
mother's unfocused stricken gaze.
In sleep
they gather purpose,
strength.
The sea comes clear.

Once I too slept like that.
I was fifteen,
and I was growing stronger in my sleep.

I kept myself
and my cheap radio tuned low
to Elvis, Roy Orbison,
the Everlys:

Well,

what're we gonna tell your mama,
what we gonna tell your pa

long sigh of *Daddy's home*

Come   with me
to   the sea
the sea   of love

Come join me baby
in an endless sleep

and
I can't tell you
how much I love you

Then, and still, I dream
about my drowning at my parents' hands,
of me, the champion swimmer
kicking free,
stroking hard deep waters
and dolphining toward treasure,
out of danger.

Those years, my white bed
a beach like this.
Sleeping, I heard the roar of surf,
tides of the equinox
inside my private ear.
A beach
all hushed in the long dreams of survivors.

3. *Albuquerque, New Mexico; July, 1985*

I write far from any coast,
this afternoon too hot to move.
Inside our desert house,
Caleb sleeps in between
summerschool mornings and his evening job.
He is fifteen.
He lengthens out.
His biceps grow.
Lately,
he hugs our old cat, whispers to her,
Never die. He asks

all questions I can't answer,
finds the pain no one, not even I
could shield him from. Sometimes
he thinks I love his brother more than him.

Tonight,
seven to closing time,
he'll serve up Rocky Road,
Banana Split Supreme,
Peach Melba Fantasy to neighbor kids
and drug-wracked strangers, all alike.

Afternoons,
he keeps his Walkman on while he's asleep.
Oceans of rock and roll wash through his head.

July 31, 1985
Night of the Blue Moon